I WANT TO BE A
PARAMEDIC

By Joanna Brundle

Written by:
Joanna Brundle

Edited by:
William Anthony

Designed by:
Danielle Webster-Jones

All facts, statistics, web
addresses and URLs in this
book were verified as valid
and accurate at time of writing.
No responsibility for any
changes to external websites
or references can be accepted
by either the author or publisher.

CONTENTS

PAGE 4   **Hello, I'm Peter!**

PAGE 6   **What Will I Do?**

PAGE 8   **How Will I Help People?**

PAGE 10   **Where Will I Work?**

PAGE 12   **What Will I Wear?**

PAGE 14   **What Equipment Will I Use?**

PAGE 16   **How Will I Travel Around?**

PAGE 20   **Where Could I Work around the World?**

PAGE 22   **Let's Pretend**

PAGE 24   **Glossary and Index**

FIRST AID

Words that look like <u>this</u> can be found in the glossary on page 24.

HELLO, I'M PETER!

Hello, I'm Peter! When I grow up, I want to be a paramedic. You could be one too! Let's find out what this job will be like.

I want to be a paramedic so that I can help people that might have had an accident or be feeling very poorly. I will be an important part of my <u>community</u>.

Did you know that anyone from around the world can become a paramedic?

WHAT WILL I DO?

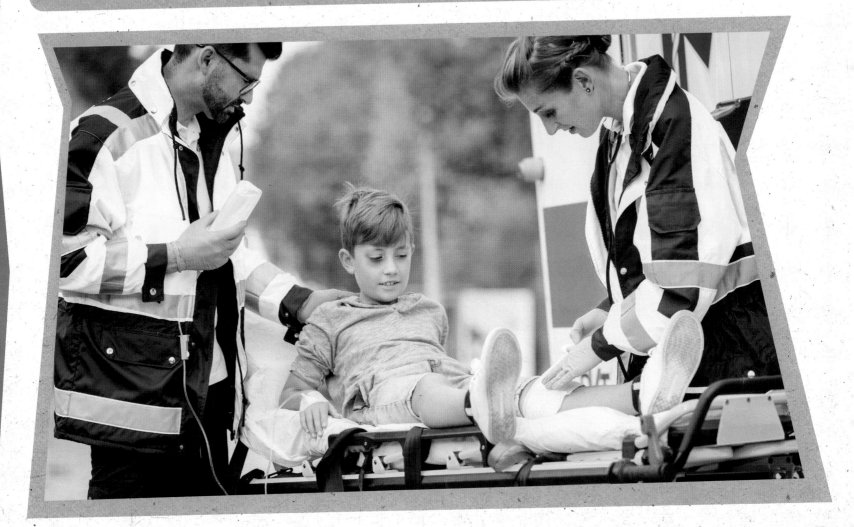

I will look after people who need <u>emergency</u> care.

I will give the <u>patient</u> the medicine and treatment they need until they can be seen by a doctor.

I will decide if the patient needs to go to hospital. If they do, I will look after them on the journey.

If I drive the ambulance, I will get to the patient or hospital as quickly as possible. Acting quickly saves lives.

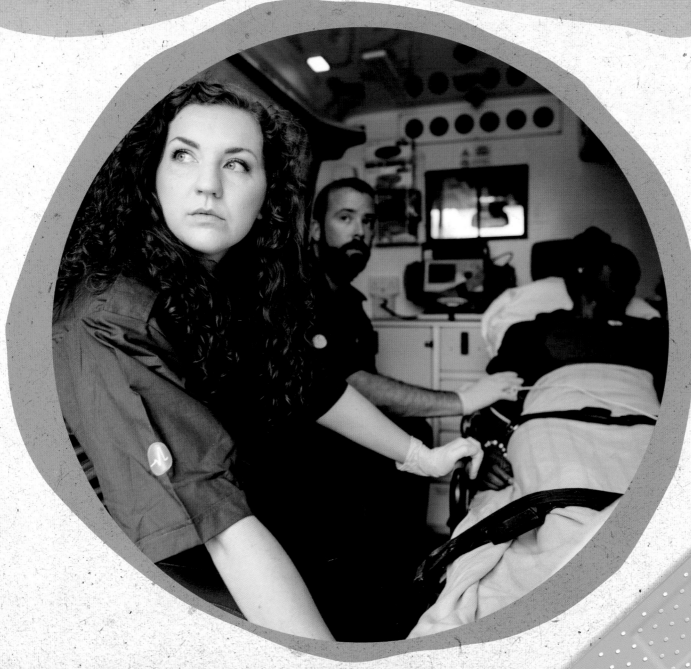

HOW WILL I HELP PEOPLE?

If there is an emergency, people can make an emergency telephone call for help. If an ambulance is needed, I might be one of the paramedics sent to help.

Paramedics respond to emergencies at any time of the day or night.

Paramedics deal with all sorts of emergencies. I might go to a traffic <u>collision</u> or to a fire. The patient might be someone who is in pain or finding it hard to breathe.

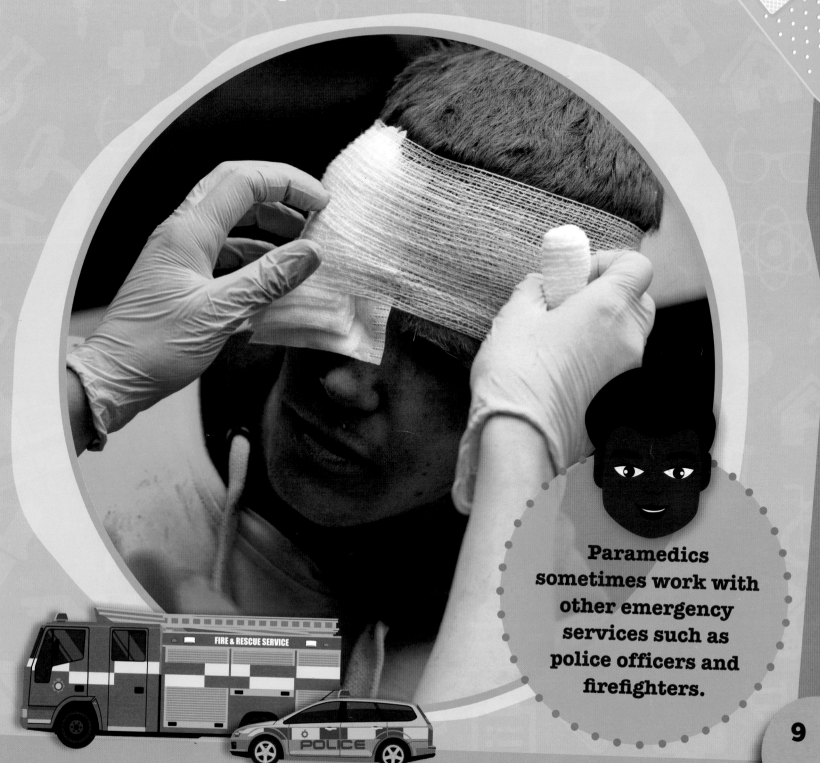

Paramedics sometimes work with other emergency services such as police officers and firefighters.

FIRE & RESCUE SERVICE

POLICE

WHERE WILL I WORK?

Emergencies can happen anywhere. I might be called to help at someone's house, on a motorway or in a town centre. Some paramedics work where there are large crowds of people, such as concerts or sporting events.

The emergency telephone number in the UK is 999. In most countries, 112 works too.

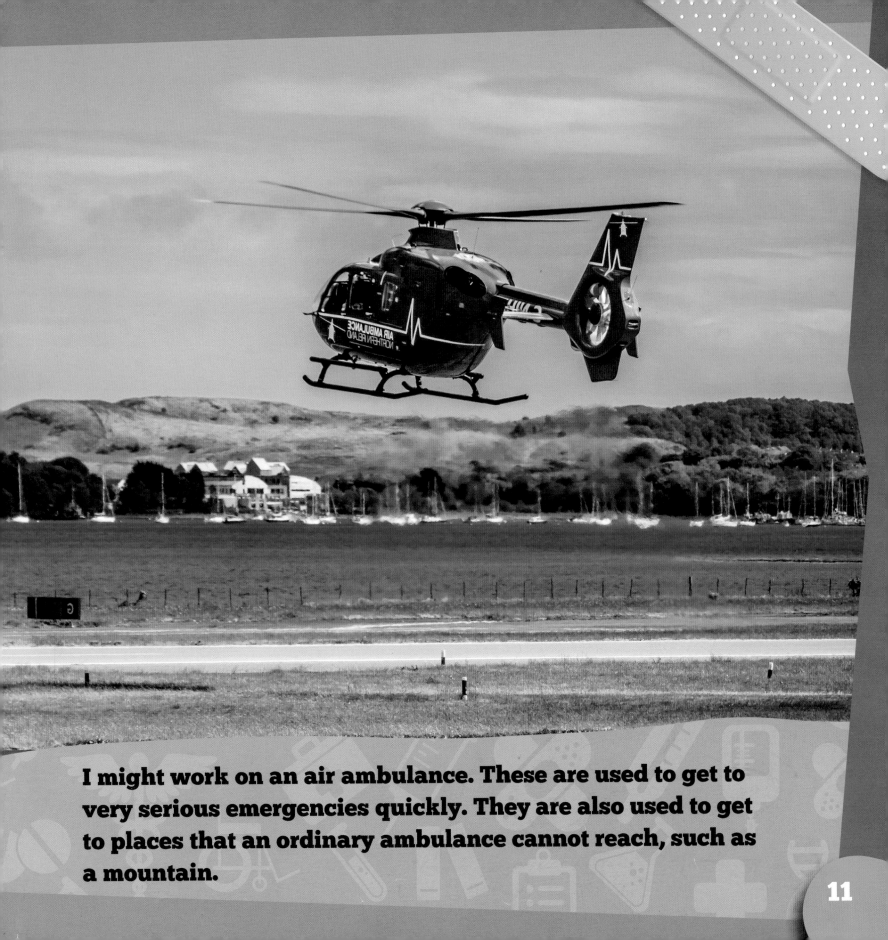

I might work on an air ambulance. These are used to get to very serious emergencies quickly. They are also used to get to places that an ordinary ambulance cannot reach, such as a mountain.

WHAT WILL I WEAR?

I will wear trousers, a shirt and a vest or jacket. The vest or jacket is brightly coloured and has special stripes. It will help me to be seen in the dark or in bad weather.

Uniforms help people to spot paramedics.

Stripes

I will also wear a tough pair of boots. They will be made of strong materials so that I can work anywhere. If I ride a bicycle, I will wear a helmet.

Paramedics sometimes work in dangerous places, so their uniforms have to be tough.

WHAT EQUIPMENT WILL I USE?

In my bag, I will carry lots of equipment, such as gloves, bandages and medicine. There will be even more equipment in the ambulance.

Oxygen mask

Gloves

Some patients will need an oxygen mask to help them breathe.

14

Radio

A defibrillator is used to help a patient whose heart is not working properly.

I will use a <u>stretcher</u> on wheels to move patients to the ambulance. I will use a radio to give the hospital information about the patient.

HOW WILL I TRAVEL AROUND?

I will usually travel to emergencies in an ambulance. Sometimes I will use an ambulance car. These cars carry life-saving equipment, just like ambulances. However, they cannot be used to take a patient to hospital.

I might use a bicycle to reach an emergency. Paramedics on bicycles can sometimes get to an emergency faster than an ambulance because they don't get caught in traffic.

The paramedic's equipment is carried in these bags.

AMBULANCES

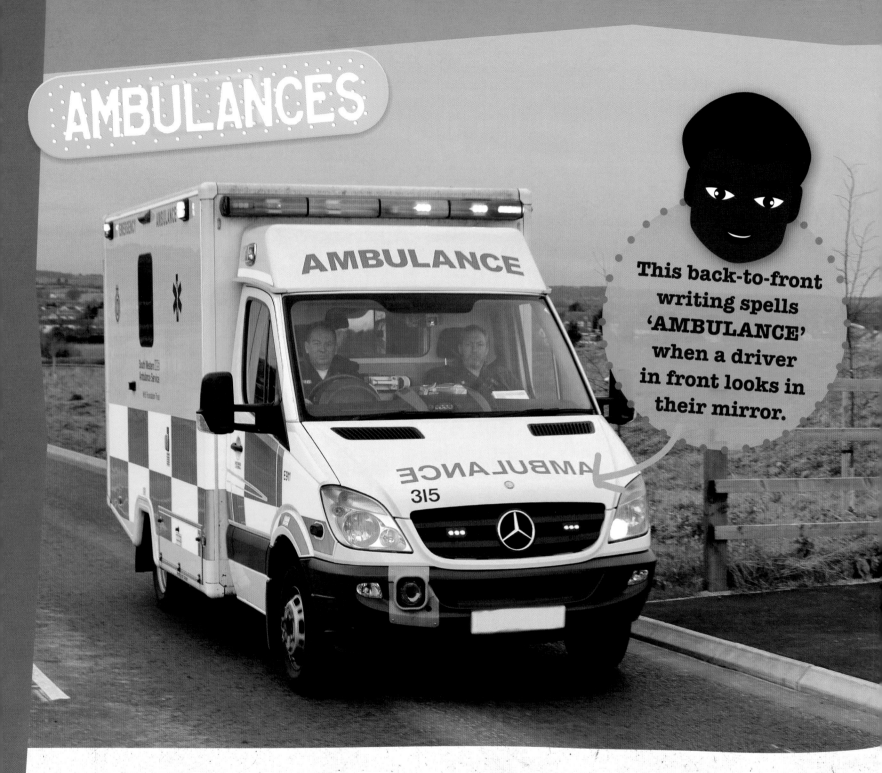

This back-to-front writing spells 'AMBULANCE' when a driver in front looks in their mirror.

The bright colours and markings on an ambulance help it to be seen easily. The flashing blue lights and loud siren warn people to get out of the way.

The ambulance has a special lift at the back. The stretcher is wheeled onto the lift, raised up and then wheeled in. Inside, there is space for the stretcher and a seat for the paramedic.

WHERE COULD I WORK
AROUND THE WORLD?

BNPB

RUANG FLAMBOYAN

This medical centre in Indonesia was set up after a <u>tsunami</u>.

I might work as part of an international emergency team. These teams help people in countries where there have been disasters, such as floods, or outbreaks of serious <u>diseases</u>.

Some paramedics work in <u>remote</u> places such as oil platforms in the middle of the sea. Others travel with scientists or volunteers on <u>expeditions</u> to places such as Antarctica and Nepal.

LET'S PRETEND

Let's work together. You can be the paramedic and I'll be the patient. Let's pretend I've fallen off my bike and hurt my leg. What equipment do you think you will need? Write a list.

Paramedics have to keep careful notes about every patient they look after. Write down when I was ill, what was wrong and what you did to help.

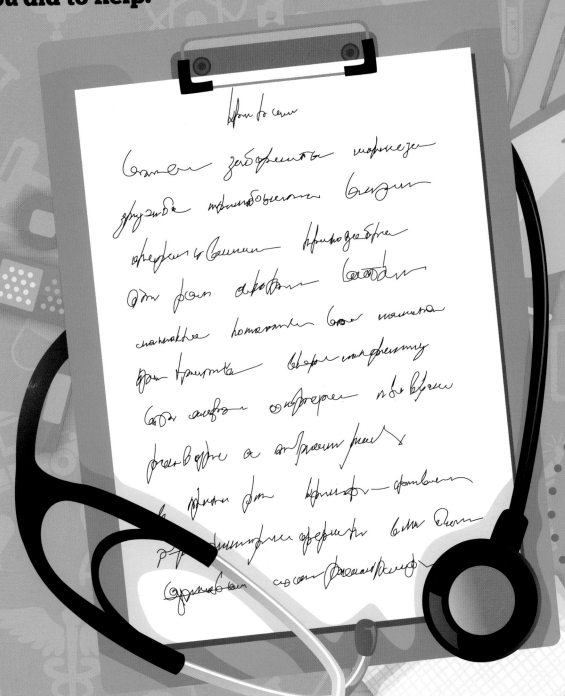

What do you think would be the best thing about being a paramedic?

GLOSSARY

COLLISION	a crash involving two or more objects
COMMUNITY	a group of people who live and work in the same place
DISEASES	illnesses that cause harm to the health of a person
EMERGENCY	a dangerous situation that requires action
EXPEDITIONS	journeys made by groups of people for a specific reason, such as exploration
PATIENT	a person who receives medical care or treatment
REMOTE	far away from people
STRETCHER	a piece of equipment used for carrying or moving an injured person
TSUNAMI	a very large wave in the ocean, usually caused by an earthquake, that causes flooding on land

INDEX

air ambulances 11
ambulance cars 16
ambulances 7–8, 11, 14–19
communities 5

defibrillators 15
emergencies 6, 8–11, 16–17, 20
emergency services 9
equipment 14–17, 22

medicines 6, 14
stretchers 15, 19
uniforms 12–13
vehicles 7–8, 11, 13–19, 22